The Missing Hamster

Written by Abi Wainwright
Illustrated by Jenny Palmer

Meet Sanjay and Annika.
They are experts at hunting for clues. Little Krishnan likes to help.

They are the Hunter Kids!

One day, they got a new friend – with paws, whiskers and bright little eyes!

It was a hamster called Scampers.

The Hunter Kids made a maze for Scampers with toy bricks. It had tunnels, paths and rainbows.

Sanjay carefully put Scampers into the maze.

She ran up and down ...

... in and out ...

... here and there!

Krishnan ran over, stamping his feet. Scampers hid.

"Krishnan, be careful!" cried Annika.

When they looked, Scampers was not there!

"Where is she?" Sanjay asked, peering into a tunnel.

"Do not fear!" said Annika. "We are the Hunter Kids!"

"I will get the spy kit!" said Sanjay.

"How did she get out?" asked Annika.

"Over here – look!" said Sanjay.
"A gap!"

"Aha!" said Annika. "That gap is right by …"

"… the bottom shelf!" shouted Sanjay. The Hunter Kids looked, but could not see Scampers.

Annika spotted a trail of sawdust. It went to the toy trains.

Sanjay looked in the tunnels and sheds ...

... with no luck.

Suddenly, Krishnan laughed. "A bit of pear!"

"How did that get there?" asked Sanjay.

"Hamsters keep food in their cheeks!" said Annika. "Did Scampers drop some?"

They saw a seed near the teddy bear …

… and grains by the armchair.

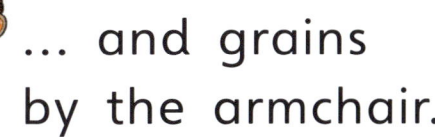

"Here she is!" cried Sanjay.

They all gave Scampers a stroke, and some yummy pear!